MW00928900

Loving, Hoping, Believing

Poetry to live by

Mark Tedesco

Copyright© 2012 by **Academia Publishing**

All rights reserved by the author. No part of this publication may be reproduced, stored in a retrieval system or transmitted in any form or by any means electronic, mechanical, photocopying, recording or otherwise, without the prior written permission of the author.

ISBN: 978-1-105-57833-5

Standard Copyright License

First Edition

Published in the United States of America by
Academia Publishing

To John Serrato
Who showed me how to love

Table of Contents

Chapter 1

Loving

Gratitude

Beyond earth and sea and sky
Is the love I bear for you
It only grows with the passing of time
Deeply rooted and true

I never expected to find a man
With your quality of heart
You are able to love me for who I am
The whole, and not just part

Gratitude is what I feel
When I think about your face
Knowing that what we have
Is only the first taste

Though I long that what binds us
Reach its fulfillment now
Step by step, I walk along
Keeping my silent vow

This love is a gift since it is bigger than us
It transcends even space and time
It fills my heart, my confidence grows
It is truly something sublime

I want to express my gratitude now
For coming into my life
And changing forever the heart where you dwell
Giving peace where there once was strife

How

How you crept into my heart
And became the center of my life
I know not how it happened
But I am certain that you are

How you loved without a plan
No agenda, just your heart
I know not how you did it
But I am certain of your love

How you saw me through and through
And embraced all that was there
You taught me how to love
Myself, you, and all

Your love burns in me still
Joy when I think of you
Knowing you carry me now
Within your great and loving heart

Today

I think I love you more today
Than I ever did in the past
I feel you growing within my heart
How long will this feeling last?

I think you are more a part of me
Than I ever thought possible before
I always knew that you were my rock
But now you give me more

True love makes two persons one
This I always believed
But as I sense you within my soul
I almost feel relieved

For once I feared that our promise
Over time would no longer hold true
But now I see its fulfillment
As I find myself in you

Is this just my imagining,
That your love grows in my heart?
You are keeping your promise
And I will do my part

More

More than earth and sea and sky
Is the love I bear for you;
I can think of nothing greater than
What binds us now anew

What I encountered on that day
When I first saw your face
I had no idea of
What eventually took place

What had come before shrunk in size
What lay ahead, the same;
The present, filled with you
My heart, you did inflame

And now I can say, what matters most
Is what I have with you
"Our special deal" of which you spoke
It even now rings true

The moon and stars, of you they speak,
The sky and earth and sea
They make no sense unless I admit
This love, it is the key

Right Love

Love was just a concept
Until I met you that day
An idea that I could define
But not point to where it lay

Love was just a feeling
Until you came across my way
It would come then leave again
But you made your love stay

You were quiet, your words were few
But you showed me with your life
Your actions were the teacher
My heart was not in strife

I miss you now but you promised
That the love would never end
You never lied or bent the truth
So to you my prayer I send

The love that you showed me
I carry in my heart
I know you are with me now
As I do my part

To share that love you gave me
To not keep it for myself
This is what you taught me
By simply being yourself

All

I love you with all my heart and soul
With all my mind, it's true
There is nothing greater that I could have
Than to always be with you

I love you more than I can say
My words always fall short;
I want to show you how I feel
But my attempts contort

So here it is, this heart of mine
I give to you today;
Look inside and you will find
What I cannot quite convey

This thing called love consumes me now
And also gives me life;
It unites my heart and soul and mind
Where before there was only strife

Thank you for who you are for me
And for who you will become;
I will forever live in gratitude
That to your love I did succumb

You

The smile on your face
The sparkle in your eye
The way you hold my hand
I feel so secure

The way you look at me
The joy you make me feel
The peace, no matter what
I feel between us now

The gift you are to me
The way you hold me to you
You share with me your love
You fill my life with joy

You are everything to me
A love without an end
I give to you my heart
I will always live for you

Took

You took away my fear
You showed me how to love
You looked me in the eyes
You saw the man I am

You're always at my side
Your heart that makes mine strong
I know you're here with me
For your embrace I long

I would give my all
To have you one more time
Our secret pact, our deal
Our bond without an end

I trust in what you said
Our lives would be as one
I believe you spoke the truth
My fear is all but gone

You went away today
I no longer see your face
My heart is broken, yet I know
Your promise is still true

Showing

You showed me what a pure heart is
That doesn't ask return
It seeks more the other's good
From your heart I learn

You love me and I love you
This to all is clear
And yet I want you with me now
You take away my fear

You went away, I see not your face
Not all can understand
How I love you and you love me
You will always be my man

Time and distance, not even death
Can take away this love
I can feel your burning presence now
Looking at me from above

I trust your words, promises too
That we would always be as one
My life is different, yet the same
Because my heart you won

Show

You show me how to love
By the way you live your life
No questions, no conditions
Never any strife

You show me how to live
Neither calculating nor small
You take it on in one embrace
Never fearing any wall

You show me how to risk
All that I am for love
My life is changed forever
Now guided from above

I feel you are with me
Though I want to feel you more
Love *has* to be forever!
I know it in my core

I place my trust in what has been
In what still will be revealed
As long as you are with me
My heart with yours is sealed

Express

Baby, I can't even think of words to say
To express what I feel in my heart
To say "I love you" is not enough
For me, it's just the start

You are the heavens for me now
The sun and moon above
And the stars are but windows
To the brightness of our love

What is it that binds us even now?
Can anyone understand?
I can't explain it but it's true
I know you are my man

Whatever happens, this remains
In the changing world, this stays:
That in our hearts, our special love
Will increase all our days

And after this our time on earth
Will it endure even then?
If anything is true, it must
True bonds will have no end

And so I hope in life today
I hope in the beyond as well
I see more heaven in your eyes
Than my words can ever tell

This Much

I never thought I could love this much
My heart is about to burst
I dreamt of this, but never thought
I could fathom such a thirst

You came into my life one day
Unplanned, unexpected, but real
You grew within me without my seeing
What your true love could heal

How I know this love is great
Is that sometimes it feels like pain
And yet it leads towards happiness
Where our bond will never wane

It is a road, this feeling
This conviction, which keeps me with you
I'm walking now, believing
That what we have is true

What I know is what I have
And what I have is you
You have me, no matter what
But this you always knew

Happy

I am happy
When I think about your face
My heart leaps
When I feel our love

I am joyful
When I remember our times
I am at peace
When you are here

I am smiling
When I know you are with me
I am content
My heart in yours

I am certain
You are part of me
I am serene, knowing
I am part of you

New Year

On this last day of the year
I want to say to you
That I am grateful you're in my life
Past and future too

The joys and sorrows we had till now
Continue in my heart
And I'm so thankful for the love
That from us will never part

It's such a gift to be with you
And you with me right now
No words can tell you what I feel
Nor describe exactly how

You are a gift to me this year
This day, forevermore
Your presence gives me courage, strength
My heart with yours does soar

I Cede

I love you more than words can speak
More than my actions can tell
I don't know how to express this thing
Between us, but you know so well

I only hope you see within my heart
And behold this enduring bond
I want to live my life for you
Hesitation and doubt, be gone

This road of life has taken its turns
I know not where it will lead
But I am certain that I will be with you then
My heart, to yours, I cede

Matters

You taught me what really matters
Not by what you said
You showed me what is important
It is by your example that you led

You showed me how not to worry
About things I can't control
You knew that things would work out
If peace be in my soul

You knew you would be with me
Every day that I would live
You knew I would love you forever
That to you, myself, I would give

I continue living this way
You dwelling in my heart
I am so happy that you are with me
That not even death can part

When

Though I cannot say precisely
The day you entered my heart
I can say with certainty
You have become an essential part

Before we met my life was fine
There was nothing that I sought
I was neither expecting nor looking for
The magic that you brought

I was not aware during that time
What was growing from within
That you were becoming part of me
That my love you would win

Looking back, there are many things
I would change now if I could
But there is one thing I am certain of
You are my heart for good

I know

You used to always tell me
That you love me more than I'll ever know
Baby, I know

You used to always look at me
As if you could see everything inside
You did see

You used to always hold my hand
As if we fit together just right
We did fit

You used to always say my name
As if I belonged somehow to you
I do belong

I never really expressed to you
That you had become my life
You are my life

Deep

It is in the measure that you love
That you can feel the pain
It's as if the deepness of the one
Returns to you again

It is in the measure that you feel
That you have joy and sadness too
As if one prepares the way
And the other, one's heart, makes new

It is in the measure that you live
That you experience all these things
The one without the other
Neither joy nor sadness brings

When your capacity is greater
Hardship is not the foe
Joy and sorrow are but tools
Since these things make your heart grow

Why

Why is it that when I say "I love you"
It doesn't begin to convey
What I feel deep inside me
I don't know how to say

Why is it that when I think of you
I feel so safe and secure
As if I have you forever
Of this my heart is sure

Why is it that when I long for you
I feel both joy and pain
Happy that you are with me now
Sad until I see you again

Why is it that when I see your face
Nothing else do I need
Your embrace is enough for me
This love my heart does lead

Certain

Though I sometimes feel distracted
You are never far from mind
You have changed my life forever
In you my joy I find

When I look back I see what was
There will be many changes still
Yet I am certain of just one thing
Your love my heart will fill

Sometimes I am frightened
Of what my life may bring
You give me confidence to face it all
Since to you my heart does cling

I find my strength in what I'm sure of
I am certain most of all
That what is true, and has begun here
Will keep growing, never stall

I want to tell you: thank you
For becoming part of me
Who you are is the greatest gift
This love will always be

Hold

I feel a gentle hold on my heart
Something I can barely detect
It's almost like a whisper but more
I can't put words on it yet

When I silence my mind and look within
I can see more clearly than before
That this quiet voice within my soul
Is leading to something more

What is this that I sense within my chest?
A thing that I never felt
It's the quiet gift you placed there one day
When my hand in yours you held

Capacity

Though my love for you has helped me see
The capacity of my heart
You give me joy and sorrow too
From me, please, never depart

Your love for me has somehow enlarged
My ability to love you back
And if I could do it over again
There is nothing that I would lack

Our love has somehow transformed my being
Now everyone can I embrace
Your love and mine are united now
As I am caught up in your grace

Tell

Baby I want to tell you I love you now
Just I've done in the past
The words never grow old somehow
I know that what binds us will last

When I feel you close my heart is at peace
I can face anything coming my way
I know I'm in you, and you in me
Together each hour of the day

I cannot imagine a greater gift than this
When we became part of one another
I look forward to what the future may bring
Since I'll face it with you, my lover

Change

I never would have guessed the change you would bring
The revolution you ignited in my heart
I could not imagine the impact you would have
As you transformed me, part by part

I could never fathom a love such as yours
Which would expand and infuse my very soul
You never asked for anything for yourself
A pure love between us was your goal

I never would have realized how your love filled my being
I'm unable to say just when it began
I'm amazed what your presence in my life has become
You are changing me into a better man

Mark Tedesco

Gift

How it happened, I cannot explain
But I'm thankful you're in my heart
As things change and people fade
From there you will never part

You lodged yourself, I know not how
Inside my heart and soul
Every day I live I think of you
Together we are one whole

This love between us, unexpected gift
My life will never be the same
Since now I live it, not just for me
Our bond will never wane

Incomplete

If I tell you that I love you
It sounds so incomplete
Expressing what you mean to me
Is an impossible feat

If I show you how I love you
Even my actions fall short
You are so much more than word or act
Or expression of any sort

So I can only stand before you:
Look into my eyes and my heart
Perhaps when you gaze within me
You will begin to see this part

A piece of me belongs to you
I tell you, it always will
You have become a part of the man I am
Since your love, my heart, does fill

Love

Baby, I love you with all my heart
With all my mind, it's true
Together or apart, it remains the same
That I belong to you

We met, unaware of what life would bring
It was not according to our plan
Some things changed, others remain
Yes, you are my man

What lies ahead is the unknown;
There is one thing of which I am sure
My heart in yours and yours in mine
Forever will this endure

Longing Today

I was longing to be with you today
But you were just beyond my reach
I wanted to hold you in my arms
I wanted time and space to breach

But you are there and I am here
It's like part of me is inside of you
Two bodies yet one life we share
I know this must be true

Your words echo in my mind today
That the love that is in my heart
Cannot be removed by anything
Since it has been there from the start

No matter what time and space separate
True love can conquer all
My heart in yours and yours in mine
Between us there is no wall

Yes I long to be with you today
But I feel you within me now
Your voice, your face, your heart do speak
Inside me, I know not how

Glad

I saw your face today
And you made me glad

I looked into your eyes today
As if I never had

I saw your heart today
I no longer felt alone

Something melted within me today
Which was once like stone

I felt your hand today
Grasping mine on the way

I felt at one with you today
Though I wanted you to stay

I held you in my arms today
Having no words to speak

I felt your heart against mine today
The one that I seek

You went away today
But I didn't feel sad

You left your love with me today
This makes me feel glad

Real Love

Real Love is made by choices
Not just feelings of the heart
It moves one to decisions
It changes one from the start

Love makes me see differently
Since there are no longer one but two
What he lives becomes my life also
I take on another view

Love that remains just feelings
Get swayed, tossed by the breeze
Life's changes it doesn't withstand
Opportunities it does not seize

Instead love that grows, increases
In feelings, yes, but more
It consists of a direction
It points me to a door

It leads me to the heart
Of another that becomes mine
It makes me see what is inside
His concerns, to me, do bind

So I choose to make these decisions
Making my life, with his, one
Because this for me is happiness
This is how love is won

I want a love that lasts
Not one that fades in the night
One that I can build my life on
This true love is my light

So I keep my eye on the person
The one who has conquered my heart
And build with him together
That we, from one another,
May not part

Whole

To see deeply within another
To behold all their strengths and weaknesses
To grasp everything this person is
And is not;
To love it all
Is no small thing

To see myself within another
To behold the good I have done, and what I have not
To grasp the man that I am
And where I fall short;
To love all of myself
Is no small thing

To embrace partly another
To accept their positives but not their faults
To change the person they are
And what they will become;
To love their potential
This is a small thing

Mark Tedesco

Promise of Love

I believe in the promise of love
Though I admit, more often that not
The happiness that I expected
Was not what this love has brought

I believe in the goodness of life
Though sometimes, I do have to admit
That what I expected was not given
And I struggled, and tried to accept it

I believe in the relentless desire
My heart points out the way
The answer is there, within me:
Goodness and kindness,
It is there
That they lay

43

Mark

I never guessed that day, long ago
When I met you and felt that spark
That it would change me deep inside
Your love has left its mark

I saw your face, it was aglow
As if everything else was dark
Your life and mine became as one
Your love has left its mark

I knew back then, as I know even now
The truth of their remark
When they would see the bond we have
Your love has left its mark

I think about the loves before
To you, they seem so stark
The love between us, greater still
Your love has left its mark

Choice

The bond with you is just as firm
As the decision that I make
Sometimes I feel it stronger or less
But my love it does not shake

My attention flows, coming back once more
To what really matters to me
As I sort it out, I realize again
That yours I want to be

Thoughts and feelings may swirl around
Distractions fill my mind
Yet through it all I am sure
To yours my heart will bind

My choice is you, and I am yours
In a way I can't explain
But I know that deep within my being
This love in me does reign

Stronger

I can never seem to express to you
How much you fill my heart
And yet the urge to, overcomes
The hesitation on my part

What you always meant to me
I cannot seem to express
Look into my eyes right now
And see if you can guess

The bond you planted in my heart
Has never ceased to grow
It's stronger now than it was before
This gift you did bestow

I know now what I could never see
Nor understand until today
This thing that cannot be expressed in words
Will never pass away

Fill

I feel secure just knowing that
You are at my side
The bond between us, stronger still
That love which is our guide

And if I could choose just one more time
The choice would be the same
I'd wish that love I found in you
This bond which has no name

Your quality of heart, you know
Struck me in the past
You integrity and honor too
For me are unsurpassed

I am grateful I have known you
As I know and love you still
Your life and mine are intertwined
Your heart, mine, does fill

Chapter 2

Hoping

You Taught Me

You taught me how to love
Now show me how to live
Would that I could see your face
To you my heart I give

You taught me how to love
Now show me how to see
That what you gave me endures still
Deep inside of me

You taught me how to love
You show me even now
That the bond that began between us
Is like a sacred vow

I know not the moment
You became part of me
My heart in yours, yours in mine
No longer "I' but "we"

I feel you still present
I need you to be here
My angel, my lover, my friend
You remove all my fear

No longer is the future
A lost or lonely way
Because you will be there with me
Just as you are today

Possibilities

Sadness can be longing
Or a prison holding me back
It can free me to look beyond
Or simply block my way

Sadness can be a door
Opening to where I know not
Or it can lock me in
Turning me back to myself

Sadness can be a road
Leading to greater things
Or it can enclose me
Weighing my spirit down

I see a choice before me
Sadness as hope or sorrow
I choose to trust a plan
That is greater than what I imagined

Promise

The look in your eyes
The simplicity of your heart
The grasp of your hand
Keep your promise

The sound of your voice
Your laugh as you smile
The security of your presence
Keep your promise

The way you make me feel
My rock and refuge, my man
The one who will always be there
Keep your promise

Together with me now
Different from before
But enduring as we vowed
Keep our promise

Mark Tedesco

Thinking, Feeling

Sometimes I don't know what to think
But I do know how I feel
The big picture sometimes doesn't make sense:
In my heart I know what is real

At the moment when I've got it all figured out
Suddenly there's a change in the plan
My ideas are tossed in the air once more
I start again from where I began

Knowing why things happen this way
Is not given me to possess
I can rebel or accept the way things are
Curse, or I can bless

In the end how I live is a choice I can make
To be open to this gift that is life
And to realize there is something greater than myself
I can be in harmony, or be in strife

Awoke

I awoke this morning
Longing to hear your voice
I almost expect to get your call
My heart then to rejoice

But what I heard was silence
Oppressive to my heart
I miss you so much baby
But I'm trying to do my part

If I didn't have a little faith
This would all be too much
All I have is the belief that
You are present in that hush

What is most important
Has been all changed around
I want to live for you, for love
To you my heart is bound

I cannot deny the sorrow
But yet, I look to you
I'm so grateful you are part of me
That what we have is true

I understand not the plan
That has led to this strange place
But I choose to trust it, since you are there
Sustaining me by grace

Embrace

Though I feel longing in my heart
To be near you all the time
Somehow I feel you close
That everything will be fine

The other night you told me
I could feel it magically true
That not only will everything be O.K.
But it's really O.K. now too

Everyone keeps telling me
What a great gift is our love
That nothing can dare to separate
It's like a miracle from above

So day by day I will learn to trust
What I know in my mind is true
That what has bound us together until this time
Will continue, though as something new

Your embrace continues to surround me
You know you are forever my man
Hold me, as I hold you, tightly now
My head, my heart and my hand

Thankful

Blue sky, bright sun, flowers
Shimmering stars, faithful moon
Strong trees, rejoicing birds
Little dog, bright fish

Friendship love, romantic love
Friends like family, embraces
Capacity to feel deeply
One special enduring love

Faith connection, giving meaning
An unfolding plan, day by day
Never alone, no matter what
The path continues, beckons

Grateful heart, lasting hope
Knowing its destiny is good
Daring to love forever
Thankful for what is being given

The Man I Am

What really matters to me this day
Is what you taught me to be true
That the man I am, and the bonds I make
Make my life become something new

I would worry about many things
Especially what I could control not
And sometimes lose sight of the most precious
That thing my heart always sought

To become the man I could admire
To love deeply, and be loved in return
These are the two things that you taught me
Each day this I seek to re-learn

Sometimes

Sometimes I wonder why I could never see
What was staring me in the face
That your love was all I wanted
Given to me by grace

I was looking out there, far and wide
Driven by something I sought to find
Grasping at what appeared but was not real
It was mostly in my mind

All that time I looked, and you were here
Standing by my side
Loyal, loving, committed
To my heart you never lied

Sometimes I wish I had another chance
To love you with all my soul
In the meantime, here I am
With you I feel whole

Before

What went before is sacred now
I didn't realize it at the time
That the happiest day I ever had
With you it was sublime

Sometimes I want to live again
The time I spent with you
I want to relish every second more
The time we had, it flew

And yet you have not abandoned me
Nor have I abandoned you
Our love can endure anything
I know, because it's true

What I now look forward to
As I am aware of your love
Is a life of joy and happiness
With you watching me from above

Essential

What is the essential thing in life
That surpasses all other things?
Is it when I reach my hopes and dreams
And the contentment that this brings?

Or is it to find the perfect love
Man or woman, it may be
And make a home, a life, together
And live in this harmony?

What if it's nothing outside of myself
That is the prize above all this?
What I love, and the man I am
Could this be the source of bliss?

That which is crucial doesn't fade
It doesn't disappear over time
How I love and who I am
Lasts and is sublime

Hope

You face is what gives me hope
Your smile lives in my heart
I carry you within me now
From me please never depart

We promised to love one another then
This promise lives in us still
And as the days and years will pass
This vow I will fulfill

You show me what it is to love
I'm grateful to you for this
Hand in hand and soul in soul
With you is perfect bliss

So I look for the fulfillment
Of what has begun to grow
You are always with me
Like a blessing that,
from on high,
does
flow

Why

Why is it that sometimes I feel you so close
And other times you seem so far?
As if you are part of the person I am
And then I wonder where you are

Why is it that I know you are here
And then I just feel your loss?
At one moment I can almost see your face
And then it does not come across

Why is it that I know this love is sure
And yet doubt that you hold me still?
You promised this bond till the end of our days
I believe it, come what will

Why is it, what I know to be true
Causes happiness, followed by pain?
Could it be what I suspected all along:
That what I thought was loss, instead, was gain?

Chapter 3

Believing

Naked

I stood there naked in the square
The crowd, they stood back
My wound was present for all to see
Knowledge they did not lack

I limped, but knew not how to say
"Come to my aid, please"
I only looked at those I knew
Hoping my pain would ease

But from fear or sorrow, I do not know
No one said a word
They only looked but did not see
My voice, it was not heard

I was not angry, for my wound was great
So much that no one could mend
Perhaps what I wanted most of all
Was one I could call a friend

Was it only the pain that others could see?
The man had shrunk in size
I knew that something important had changed
Since no one would look in my eyes

I bound my wound and walked away
Knowing that I could be whole
The answer I sought was not in the square
To find it would be my goal

Tether

There is a tether
That binds my heart
To yours, beyond my sight
I feel the pulsing of your presence
You guide me in your light

There is a tether
That draws you near
Pulls me to where you are
I can almost clutch what I cannot see
You do not feel so far

There is a cord that binds
My life to yours
Beyond all human strength
Nor life nor death can change its course
Eternity its length

There is a life that ties
My being to yours
Without which I do not live
The man you are flows into me
To you myself I give

Sense

There has to be something greater
That makes sense of this thing called life:
Its opposites and contradictions
Creating harmony from strife

There has to be something more
Than I can create with my own mind
Which can take the disconnected pieces
And in one bigger picture, bind

There has to be a greater meaning
Than the one I currently decide
Which can take my failed plans and projections
And use them for my guide

There has to be a greater road
Than the one I used to foresee
Leading me to unimagined vistas
And from my own limits, set me free

Tightrope

Sometimes life is a balancing act
Despair and hope on either side
If I look down I fear losing my grip
Looking up, in a plan I can confide

Sometimes the tightrope can seem so extreme
When I look and see what's at stake
And then I remember I am not in control
My destiny my hands do not make

If I look at what I've lost or fear to lose
I feel myself quiver and fall
But when I realize what a great gift life is
I can be grateful for the happy, the sad, all

Sometimes I realize I have the power to choose;
That happiness includes hope and despair
The secret is being open to what's greater than me
Even when it doesn't seem fair

Look

The look in your eyes
The touch of your hand
The sound of your voice
I feel your love

The concern on your face
The tears on your cheeks
"It will be O.K.", you said
I believe in your love

The smile from your heart
The joy of being with you
Continue even now
Believe in my love

Edge

You brought me to the edge
Of disbelief and despair
I thought I understood your plan
But this filled me with fear

"You failed me", I told you
I meant every word
"How could you let this happen!" I cried
My love seemed unheard

"The gift that you gave me
You only take away
So what's the use of giving it?"
I ask in dismay

But the anger I was feeling
Is becoming sadness and love
Though I still don't understand
I can begin to look above

"There is a greater plan", I said
Not knowing what I meant
I fight to trust it, holding firm
This love, it won't relent

Trust

I thought I understood once
How your plan for me would unfold
Challenges to help me grow
Surrounded by those I hold

But now I understand not
I don't even know what to ask
Baffled by what you permit
I can feel my heart gasp

I can choose to believe or not
Trust or chaos before me now
Though baffled I remain
To you I make this vow

To trust though I don't understand
I choose this path once more
The mystery of this unfolding road
I feel it at my core

I rely on the truth of this plan
It is the consolation of my heart
I can't quite see, can barely grasp
But for me this is a start

Tell

They tell me the place where you now dwell
Is one of love and peace
That you have no regrets and see me still
Where happiness does not cease

They tell me that the love that has begun
If true, it has no end
That what is between us, binds us now
Nothing can ever rend

It gives me hope to know that between you and me
The connection has just begun
And when life springs to eternity
Our lives will continue as one

They tell me that life is beautiful
More amazing than what it appears
It only takes a little faith
To wipe away my tears

Supposed

It wasn't supposed to happen this way
You ought to be with me still
You promised me, I promised you
Our hearts, with love, we would fill

And yet I reach out to you
Your hand I cannot feel
I long to hear your voice right now
Forget not our special deal

I miss you now and every day
I need to feel you close
What is the connection that binds us now
That time will not oppose?

It's love plus faith this time around
Before it was only love
My heart to yours, and yours to mine
Bound together from above

Reverse

If I was there and you were here
Me looking at you now
I would want you to love and live
Just as I showed you how

I would grasp the sadness of loss
But I wouldn't want you to stay put
I would want you to continue to grow
And realize what you got

A love that began some time ago
And continues to increase with time
A bond that nothing can come between
Believe me, that you are mine

So continue to grow and live
And learn to be happy once more
Know that I am with you now
Together we will soar

To love and live, to live and love
Are the secrets our lives reveal
What binds us continues even now
Remember our special deal

So I am here and you are there
You love me, this I know
Why should it be different now?
What has started will always grow

Christmas

That which is invisible
Became something I can feel
A Presence just beyond my grasp
Yet I can sense that it is real

Chaos is the alternative
If I push it all away
Meaningless takes hold of me
If I blind myself to this way

Yet with this my acceptance
Obscure though it may be
I welcome something into my life
That makes me feel more free

A Presence that gives my life meaning
It takes the place of all my fear
Since it contains the promise
Of what my heart holds dear

What I desire more than anything,
What my heart seeks in hope and love
Does indeed have an answer
Descended down this night from above

All things right

There has to be a certain order
Greater than what I can see
Since the unfolding of my plans
Never ever comes to be

I've seen this in frustration
And even in anger too
But then I step back and realize
Another point of view

Although the plans I set in place
Have seldom come to pass
What instead has happened
Has taught me what to ask

What really is essential,
What matters most, bar none
Are the bonds of love I hold onto
And the man I can become

Before I thought I had figured out
How life would unfold in my sight
But now I've come to trust
The plan that sets all things right

Bigger Picture

Though I strive to see the bigger picture
Which you experience right now
My heart falters and my mind fails
Since I do not know quite how

I strive to believe and trust that plan
That you have finally embraced
It seemed so easy before this event
I can hardly see that I'm graced

I want to feel what I only know
To sense what I can only believe
That this bond between us, begun before,
This silence, will relieve

I can take this leap, that this love here
Can penetrate into the beyond
Binding my heart to yours, even now
I believe that you are not gone

The promises we made that day
Must endure into endless time
Our hearts are made for eternity
For me, this love is the sign

More

I love you more than words can say
I wish you were with me now
You say you are, but I reach out
And touch you, I know not how

I love you more than I ever knew
You completely fill my heart
I wish to tell you one more time
Before you have to depart

I wish we were together now
Though you say we are
And feel your loving embrace once more
Instead I see you in the stars

You often called me your angel
And now my angel you have become
Never abandon me here below
Until, where you are, I come

Beginning

I start the day knowing you are near
Loving me just like before
I feel you though I hear not your voice
I love you evermore

This bond that began some time ago
Has endured this trial by storm
And I will never let you go
Though this take another form

I want what we have had before
Please be with me right now
All I have left is faith in you
And in our mutual vow

Believe in me, I believe in you
In this I place my trust
That what binds us here will have no end
If life has meaning, it must

Wrapped Up

Sometimes I feel the love and pain
But one day it will just be love
While I have you and yet have you not
You are here and yet above

I see your face yet touch it not
Your presence I can feel
My heart is burning for you now
My God, this must be real

You are here, just like before
We are standing side by side
And yet I cannot quite hear
Your whispering voice inside

I love you and you love me
Of this I am quite sure
Everything else may pass away
But I know this bond endures

So I place my love in what I cannot see
Your love that is in my heart
Knowing that what had bound us once
From us will not depart

The Promise

Sometimes I need to trust in what I cannot see
To make sense of what I can
Sometimes I need to grasp what I cannot feel
So that I can understand

Sometimes I need to go beyond myself
Since I can't figure it all out
I can confide in what is greater than me
Or I can remain in doubt

I have a sense of where the truth lies
I can feel it under my skin
It is the fulfillment of what has begun
Something growing from within

I see my heart now as a promise
Of the beauty yet to come
And what seemed as shadows until now
Are simply my doubts undone

So I open myself to this magic
That all this could possibly be true
And what I have desired and longed for
All this time
Could be found
In you

Lasting Bond

About today you never said
I'd be facing it alone
I always understood that we
Would live our lives as one

I feel sad, and happy too
When I think about your face
Wishing I had savored more
Being together in one place

Though you are there and I am here
I can never let you go
Once you entered in my heart
Forever this will grow

The love that bound me to you once
Binds me to you right now
And what I hope for on that day
Is to be with you somehow

Though life continues, I believe
That what we vowed was true
That what we had together once
Continues now in you

Though I still hold sweet memories
Of us together then
I ask you to be present now
Your love and peace please send

I thus place all my trust in you
And still believe that it is true
That this bond which has united us
Will last forever too

Mark Tedesco

Plans

You always reassured me of the goodness of life
That everything would be O.K.
I strive to believe the truth of your words
And the meaning of what you say

What has come is not what I ever had planned
And yet, I believe it all makes sense
I'm not able yet, however, to grasp it all
Especially in your absence

The plan of life is something you did not fear
You are not afraid of it still
You taught me to be open to what's beyond myself
Because I love you, I will

You show me that there is a loving plan
Not limited by what I may want
What I thought was lost, I possess even now
My heart I will doubt not

Plan

Sometimes I see a plan bigger than me
Unfolding in the circumstances of life
Other times chaos and no purpose appear
Everything seems like it's in strife

When I'm happy I can say: "There is the plan!"
When I'm sad: "It is all so unjust!"
And yet life shows they are inextricably linked
Accept one with the other, I must

I can read reality in one of two ways:
Chaos or part of a plan
Which one for me makes sense out of life,
And makes me what type of man?

My heart already knows the way to go
I can feel the tug from inside
Trust in that which is greater than me
Have faith and in the plan confide

Exchange

If I was asked to exchange my life
Instead of yours, take mine
It wouldn't take a second thought
To hand it to the Divine

If I were given a second chance
To die instead of you
I'd grab it as a precious gift
More precious than a jewel

That you might live and I might live
Is the greatest gift of all
I would not ask for more than this
Just to answer this call

But if the choice were given, that just one
Could continue on this earth
I'd hand this over to you my love
And wait for your rebirth

I love you more than life can tell
Than words can express or say
And trust in the one who put us here
To him, for us, I pray

Give

If I could give what you have given
I wouldn't hesitate at all
The love that binds us together now
Transcending any wall

If I could love as you have loved me
I would not count the cost
Your heart in mine expands it more
So I do not count the loss

If I could forgive as you have forgiven
Never holding any ill will
I'd count myself a blessed man
As my heart would be more still

If I could be as you have been
A blessing for all to know
I'd spend all my life in gratitude
Since your gift in me will grow

Close

You smiled when you saw me
You held my hand when we drove
You let me cry in your lap
You held me when I needed you

You were with me across the room
You checked in with me through the day
You shared your joys and sorrows
You made mine your own

You always said we would be O.K.
You knew the mountain would come after the valley
You were supposed to get well
But you didn't

Understand

I have to admit I don't understand
Why things happen the way that they do
I try to see logic in what I cannot control
Striving for some sort of clue

But when I look hard and try to see
What the big picture might mean instead
I end up returning where I started from;
It all doesn't fit in my head

So why things happen, I cannot explain
A mystery is the bad and the good
I can only trust in something greater than me
Finding meaning, yes this I could

So as things unfold I can open my heart
Admitting I don't know every thing
Choosing to trust in the goodness of life
Using sorrow and joy to take wing

Know

"Things were not supposed to turn out this way!"
I hear the voice in my head
I thought I understood my road
And the meaning of what you said

Instead life's different from what I thought
My plans, they went awry
It's hard to makes sense of this
I've even stopped asking why

I look ahead, I'm still unsure
How life will yet unfold
But one thing I am certain of
It won't be as foretold

The crucial thing, this I swear
Is where I place my trust
In a plan that I cannot control
Confide in this, I must

Serenity is mine to share
Or squander, if I will
The choice is mine to make once more:
To rise or go downhill

Peace can be mine if I place my trust
In what lasts and does endure
I choose this, the road to happiness
With you, of this I'm sure

I Miss You

I miss you more, I have to admit
Than I ever thought I would
I realize how much you are part of me
Be with you, I wish I could

Yet I believe that even now
You're with me and I, you
I have to count on this our bond
If the words we spoke were true

This is indeed a leap of faith
To embrace what I cannot see
And yet it seems so reasonable
To believe in what can be

I must hold onto this, you know
To embrace that love which lasts
And know that we are together now
Just as in the past

Believe

I must believe you're with me
Or none of this makes sense
Our bond must be true even now
Or is this just a pretense?

I have to believe the meaning of
What binds us then and now
Because if anything on earth is true
This must be so, somehow

I long to hear your voice sometimes
And feel your hand in mine
See you across the room and know
That everything is fine

Yet I am left with only faith
That what I believe is true
This must be enough because I want to live
My entire life with you

So I will fulfill the plan for me
If you accompany me on this road
Knowing that what bound us then
Continues to be bestowed

Fear

I am no longer afraid to die
But I am afraid to live
I only want to be with you
And to you, my heart, to give

And yet there's something greater still
That tells me there is a way
Almost a plan unfolding here
Loving, come what may

My heart and mind do battle now
Sad and full of hope
Feeling one way and knowing the other
It's faith that helps me cope

If I had no ability to accept
That which I cannot see
My longing would be frustrated
My heart no longer free

I sense that life is a promise
Saying: what you long for is true
The path is already in my heart
This love which is the clue

Mark Tedesco

Roads

There are many roads to paradise
My love for you is one
You guide me there just like a star
Your heart is like the sun

You show me the way to happiness
Far from now yet soon
Your love illuminates my path
As the light shines from the moon

I feel your warmth flowing now
As beams and rays from above
You stir my heart as once you did
Forever is this love

I thank you now for being my road
My moon, my sun, my stars
All that which we hoped for once
One day will all be ours

Acceptance

I don't think I understand your plan at all
Though sometimes I think I do
Just when the pieces fall into place
Comes undone what I think I knew

Sometimes the puzzle seems to fit
The pieces become one whole
I see the picture, all making sense
It all seems under control

But then something falls out of place
What I thought is not what is
The meaning I placed on all these things
Is not what the event says

Only by accepting what I cannot control
Can I live in the present, now
And believe that there is a greater plan
Than the one that I would allow

Goodness

Having faith in the goodness of life
Depended on my plans fulfilled
If things would unfold the way I wanted
My spirit, it would be thrilled

When things didn't happen as I forecast
I protested: "how can this be?!"
"Unjust, not right!" I said to the sky
"Isn't God my employee?"

And then one day it dawned on me
That perhaps something greater was at play
As if I could touch it, but not quite comprehend
What was guiding me on my way

What is this thing that I protest
When things are not under my command?
Perhaps I have trouble admitting to myself
That my life is in another one's hand

Depending on myself requires no trust
Only that I exert control
Over people and things, but I may find that
This effort does take its toll

It's uncomfortable to trust in one greater than me
Since I must loosen the grip on my plan
And hand over all that effort that I've made for so long
I really don't know if I can

But I've glimpsed the solution, even from afar
Of the doors that trust might open
To let go, to grasp what is greater than me
To believe that the promise is unbroken

This new way I walk, with some fear
Not knowing what the future might be
Yet the serenity is even greater still
Since it no longer
all depends
on me

Puzzle

Part of my heart died yesterday
Since it resides in you
I will move forward as life unfolds
Since that is what you taught me to do

I often hope that the puzzle of life
Its pieces, would fall into line
Yet, what I least expect occurs
Is it a plan that is not mine?

Forget the one great love, I cannot
Nor obscure the change you have wrought
I carry within me a spark, the bond so strong
You are the one I have sought

A great sign for me, your presence was
Your friendship, affection, love
I sometimes dwell in that deep valley
But I can see the highest peak above

I may not feel it, but I know
That what you brought me is here to stay
Since you are the gift that I had longed for
Thank you for being with me this day

Fair

Can I claim that I
Have had my fill,
That the joy and sorrow are now enough?
Can I stake my limit
On what I can bear?
And anything else, should I rebuff?

Could my life be different
Should I decide,
Pick and choose what I would endure?
But perhaps if I did this
Life would be less:
This love would be more insecure

If I could have chosen
The easier road
I certainly would have done so before
But my heart and mind
Would both be smaller still
And I would desire little
Or nothing more

As it is I am stretched
Beyond the limits I place
I rebel, and object: "It's not so!"
But when I can accept
A destiny greater than me
The love and the joy can both grow

Veil

Sometimes the veil seems so thin
True, or in my mind?
As if I could almost see your face
Real, or am I blind?

Sometimes you seem so far away
Other times you seem right here
Your voice, sometimes, it seems so close
Ringing in my ear

Sometimes I can almost feel your touch
You hand in my hand still
Reassuring me that all will be O.K.
Knowing that, with you, it will

Instead of eyes I have this belief
Neither touch nor sound can grasp
That what bound us then does bind us now
To this faith I firmly clasp

For Me

For me what is essential
Is this bond I have with you
Though everything may pass and change
This connection remains true

For me what really matters
Is not what I control
It's not what I hold within my hands
That can keep me feeling whole

For me what I can count on
Is this decision bound by love
To make my life be one with yours
Is what my peace is made of

For me what truly lasts
Is not what I used to think
Most of which has faded away
Except, with you, this link

Flame

There is a flame that burns deep inside
It's calm and sure and true
It does bind my heart even now
It is there that I find you

The winds may blow, but not put out
That flame which gives me life
It holds me firm, so I may face
Whatever causes strife

This flame of love and loyalty
Holds me throughout the day
As I am aware that you are here
I fear not, come what may

This gift that burns within my heart
It's peace flows to my soul
Reminding me what matters most
Is that which makes me whole